# YOU CHOOSE
BOOKS

# SNOW WHITE
and the SEVEN DWARFS

AN INTERACTIVE FAIRY TALE ADVENTURE

by Jessica Gunderson

illustrated by
Sabrina Miramon

CAPSTONE
a capstone

You Choose Books are published by Capstone Press,
1710 Roe Crest Drive, North Mankato, Minnesota 56003
www.mycapstone.com

**Library of Congress Cataloging-in-Publication Data**
Library of Congress Cataloging-in-Publication data is available on the Library of
Congress website.
978-1-5157-6943-9 (library binding)
978-1-5157-6951-4 (paperback)
978-1-5157-6954-5 (eBook PDF)

**Editorial Credits**
Michelle Hasselius, editor; Lori Bye, designer; Bob Lentz, art director;
Gene Bentdahl, production specialist

**Image Credits**
Shutterstock: solarbird, background

Printed and bound in the United States of America.
012018R   011032R

# Table of Contents

The leader steps inside and shines his flashlight on your face. "What have we here?" he says to his cronies, who have piled into the cave behind him. "A thief!"

"I'm no thief!" you protest, but the Huntsmen ignore you. They grab your arms and tie you up.

The ropes are tight around your chest. You can barely breathe. You know you are doomed. The Huntsmen cackle with laughter as they exit the cave, leaving you to die.

Late that night you wake to something pulling at your ropes. Wet noses nuzzle your arms and sloppy tongues lick your hands. The dogs! They gnaw at the rope knots until finally you are free. You and the dogs slip quietly out the mouth of the cave.

When you get outside, the night is clear. You still have to get to Snow-White, but the storm and the Huntsmen are gone.

86

## THE END

TO FOLLOW ANOTHER PATH, TURN TO PAGE 9.

You motion for the dogs to follow and move through the thick snowflakes toward the voices. Happy jumps eagerly through the snow. Doc hangs back and scratches at your leg. He's trying to tell you something, but you aren't sure what. You just keep blindly moving forward.

"Hello!" you call into the wind. "Over here!" You're not sure if they heard you. The voices are still talking. You can just make out what one of them is saying.

"I can't believe you lost our entire haul!" one man yells. "I risked my neck to rob that place!"

You freeze. You realize you've stumbled across the Huntsmen, a notorious gang of robbers. The Huntsmen scour the Arctic, stealing anything they can get their hands on. No one has been able to catch them.

"Wait. Did you hear something?" another voice says.

*Uh-oh*, you think.

"Hello!" the Huntsmen call into the wind.

Just then Sneezy lets out a giant *Achoo!* "Hush!" you tell him, but it's too late. Through the white shield of snow, you can see several dark figures moving toward you.

You have two choices — run or try to talk to them. You're not sure how fast you can go in this snow. You might be able to use the Huntsmen to find Snow-White. But they are dangerous, and there's no telling what they'll do.

TO TALK TO THE HUNTSMEN,
TURN TO PAGE 95.

TO RUN,
TURN TO PAGE 99.

You tug on the dogs' reins to turn them toward the apples. As you get closer, the crates grow more solid in shape. You reach for a red apple and try to take a bite. It's ice cold and rock hard.

"Ouch," you say. You stuff your pockets with apples. Hopefully they will warm up on your way to Snow-White. Suddenly you hear voices again. This time they are closer.

"The stash is around here somewhere," one voice says.

"Find it!" the other growls. "We stole too much to lose it now."

*Stolen apples?* you think. Of course! This is the work of the Huntsmen, a band of thieves who roam the Arctic robbing every home and village they find.

The police have been looking for the Huntsmen for years, but they always manage to stay under the radar.

You duck behind the crates and listen. From the sound of it, there are only two of them. You might be able to take them on. You gather as many apples as you can. One slips from your arms and rolls through the snow. Dopey bounds after it thinking it's a ball.

"Come back!" you hiss.

As it turns out, Dopey has done you a favor. The Huntsmen come into view, but they are distracted by Dopey. They don't notice you behind the crates. You stand, take aim, and pelt the men with the frozen apples.

TURN THE PAGE.

*Bam! Bam!* The surprised men fall over, clutching their heads. You leap from behind the apple crates and tie their hands together with your dogs' reins. You fasten the reins to the back of the sled and drag the Huntsmen behind you.

"Our leader will have your head for this!" one of them cries.

When you reach the top of the hill, you check your cell phone for a signal. It works! You dial the police and tell them you've captured two of the Huntsmen.

After some time you hear the sound of a helicopter. You wave it down, and it lands nearby. A police officer jumps out and slaps handcuffs on the two men.

"Off to jail for you," the officer says to the Huntsmen.

"We need to make another stop," you say as you climb into the helicopter. "Meteorologist Snow-White is trapped in the weather station."

"You heard him," the officer says to the pilot. "Someone's trapped in the snow."

You give yourself a little pat on the back. You certainly feel like the hero in this story.

## THE END

TO FOLLOW ANOTHER PATH, TURN TO PAGE 9.

You decide to talk to the Huntsmen. But what will you say? Suddenly you get an idea.

"Hello!" you call.

The Huntsmen charge toward you. The leader is on a huge black horse. "Where are you going, kid?" the leader asks.

"I'm looking for a treasure," you say. "Can you help me get there?"

The Huntsmen leader raises his eyebrows. "A treasure, huh?"

You nod eagerly. "Yes! I've seen it — gold, silver, and jewels! There's too much for me to carry on my own. If you help me, you can keep part of the treasure."

The leader thinks for a moment. Greed fills his eyes. "OK, kid," he says. "Show us the way."

The leader pulls you up onto his horse, and you call for the dogs to follow behind. You give the gang directions, and the posse sets off across the snowy trail. Soon you near your destination. On a small hill sits a huge mound of snow. Buried underneath is the weather station, but only you know that. You point toward the snow pile.

"There's the buried treasure!" you tell the leader. You cross your fingers and hope that Snow-White will catch on to your plan.

The Huntsmen gallop toward the station. The leader orders you to stay on the horse. He and the rest of the Huntsmen begin to dig in the snow.

"I've found something!" one Huntsman cries. "It's a glass door."

"Well, open it!" the leader orders.

The Huntsmen pull open the door and rush inside. You leap off the horse just as Snow-White runs out the door. She slams the door behind her and turns the key. The leader's face is pressed up against the glass as he pounds on the door. He and the rest of the Huntsmen are trapped. You give him a little wave.

"They won't be getting out of there for a while," Snow-White chuckles. "Thanks for coming to my rescue, Charming!"

"Nothing to it!" you say with a grin.

## THE END

TO FOLLOW ANOTHER PATH, TURN TO PAGE 9.

You whirl around and take off in the opposite direction of the Huntsmen. Doc leads the way, and Grumpy jumps onto the sled. He is protecting you. You can hear the Huntsmen chasing you, but then they stop. Phew! They must have lost you in the snow. You're safe. But now *you* are lost in a world of white. You can't see a thing.

You keep plunging through the billowing snow. The Evil Queen of Blizzards is pummeling you. You know you and the dogs should take cover, but you're nearly to the weather station. It's only an hour's trek, maybe less. Still the Evil Queen could kill you in minutes, and it's starting to get dark. **99**

TURN THE PAGE.

Suddenly you see a faint flicker of light. Could there be a house out here in the wilderness, or is it just a reflection in the snow? You could check it out, but it's in the opposite direction of the weather station.

TO CHECK OUT THE LIGHT,
GO TO PAGE 101.

TO KEEP GOING TO THE WEATHER STATION,
TURN TO PAGE 104.

You stumble toward the flickering light. If it's a cabin, the owners might help you rescue Snow-White. It's worth a try. Sure enough the light is coming from a small cottage nestled between two hills. You can't believe your luck. You pound on the door.

"Anyone home?" you call. No one comes to the door, so you peer through the frosty windows. Although the lights are on, the cottage is empty. The door is unlocked.

Inside you find a room with a large bed. The exhausted dogs jump onto the bed and settle down for a nap. You need to wait out the storm anyway, so you join them. You huddle next to Sleepy and doze off.

TURN THE PAGE.

Suddenly you wake to someone shaking you. You blink your eyes.

"Snow-White?" you say surprised. "What are you doing here?"

"I got out of the weather station just in time and have been tracking your location," Snow-White explains. "I guess *I'm* the one saving *you*."

## THE END

TO FOLLOW ANOTHER PATH, TURN TO PAGE 9.

You keep going, hoping you've made the right decision. You shake your fist in the air. "You can't stop me, Evil Queen!" you shout.

You can't feel your hands or feet. Your loyal dogs keep plunging through the snow and cold. Finally you see the weather station ahead — or at least where the weather station should be. In it's place is a huge mound of snow. You'll have to do a lot of digging to get Snow-White out.

With every bit of energy you have left, you claw at the snow. A shard of glass cuts through your glove and spots of red blood drop onto the

white snow. With dread you realize the glass walls of the weather station have collapsed under the weight of the snow.

Frantically you keep digging. At last you feel something. It is Snow-White's hand! You haul her out from under the snow.

Your friend is ice cold and isn't moving. You fear she's dead.

"No!" you scream. You kneel over her. Hot tears fall from your eyes onto her cold, blue face.

Suddenly you feel a cold hand touch your cheek. "It's OK," Snow-White's voice cuts into your sobs. "I'm alive."

You open your eyes, astonished. Snow-White slowly sits up and brushes the snow off her coat. Then she looks up at the sky. "Look!" she says. "The Evil Queen is gone."

You look up into a clear, cloudless sky. Light from the moon falls onto your face. You grin and hug Snow-White. You've survived the evil storm.

105

## THE END

TO FOLLOW ANOTHER PATH, TURN TO PAGE 9.

## CHAPTER 5

# The Many Tales of Snow White

The story of Snow White was well known throughout Germany, even before it was published by brothers Jacob and Wilhelm Grimm. Researchers believe two sisters, Jeannette and Amalie Hassenpflug, told the Grimm brothers the story.

Although Snow White is a fairy tale, it may be based on actual events. Some people believe the story is based on the life of Margaretha von Waldeck, a 16th century German countess.

When Margaretha was 17 years old, she was sent away by her stepmother to live in Brussels, Belgium. There she fell in love with Prince Phillip II of Spain, and the two planned to marry. But Margaretha's parents disapproved of the relationship. Margaretha died mysteriously at age 21, possibly after being poisoned.

Others believe the story is based on Princess Maria Sophia Margaretha Catharina von Erthal, who was born in 1725. She lived in a castle in Lohr, Germany. Mirror manufacturers during this time made elaborate mirrors that were said to "always tell the truth." Some of these mirrors had small messages inscribed in the corners. Maria Sophia's father, Prince Phillip Christoph von Erthal, presented such a mirror to Claudia, his second wife. Claudia was a harsh stepmother, so Maria Sophia ran away to the forested mountains.

In the mountains Maria Sophia came across miners from Bieber. Miners were often short and small so they could fit in narrow mining tunnels.

No one knows for certain if either story was the basis for Grimm's *Snow White and the Seven Dwarfs*. But it's not just a German story. Hundreds of stories from Norway to Mozambique to Turkey to Italy tell similar tales. Although the stories are different, each one has a jealous parent or stepparent.

In 1937 Walt Disney produced an animated film called *Snow White and the Seven Dwarfs*. In his film Disney gave the dwarfs names: Happy, Grumpy, Sleepy, Sneezy, Dopey, Doc, and Bashful. *Snow White and the Seven Dwarfs* was the first full-length animated Disney movie. The movie and the fairy tale are still loved today.

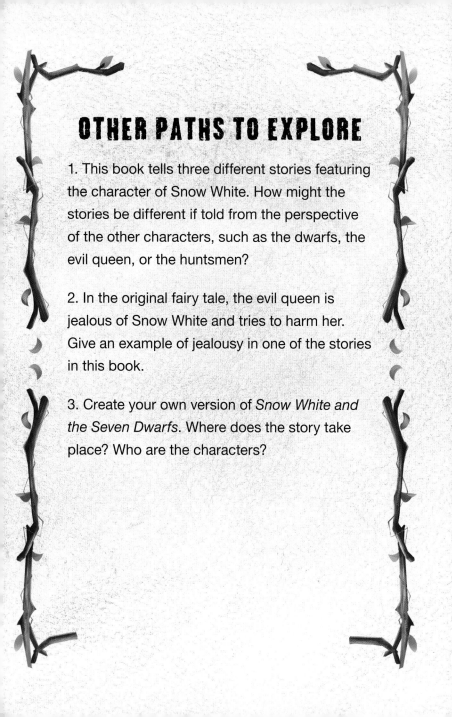

# OTHER PATHS TO EXPLORE

1. This book tells three different stories featuring the character of Snow White. How might the stories be different if told from the perspective of the other characters, such as the dwarfs, the evil queen, or the huntsmen?

2. In the original fairy tale, the evil queen is jealous of Snow White and tries to harm her. Give an example of jealousy in one of the stories in this book.

3. Create your own version of *Snow White and the Seven Dwarfs*. Where does the story take place? Who are the characters?

# READ MORE

**Cali, Davide.** *Snow White and the Seventy-Seven Dwarfs.* Plattsburgh, N.Y.: Tundra Books of Northern New York, 2015.

**Gunderson, Jessica.** *Snow White: 4 Beloved Tales.* Stories Around the World. North Mankato, Minn.: Picture Window Books, 2015.

**Leowen, Nancy.** *Seriously, Snow White Was So Forgetful!: The Story of Snow White As Told by the Dwarves.* North Mankato, Minn.: Picture Window Books, 2013.

# INTERNET SITES

Use FactHound to find Internet sites related to this book.

Visit *www.facthound.com*

Just type in 9781515769439 and go.

# LOOK FOR ALL THE BOOKS IN THIS SERIES:

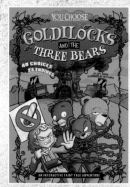

# About Your Adventure

The woods can be frightening when you are on your own. With each step you take, you feel like you're being watched. Has someone come to help you or to do you harm?

In this fairy tale, you control your fate. The seven dwarfs lead the way as you make choices to determine what happens next.

5

Chapter One sets the scene. Then you choose which path to read. Follow the directions at the bottom of the page as you read the stories. The decisions you make will change your outcome. After you finish one path, go back and read the others for new perspectives and more adventures.

# On the Run

All you can hear is your own breath as you run as fast as you can through the forest. There's something behind you. Or *someone*. You duck behind a tree. All you hear is silence now. Maybe it was just your mind playing tricks on you. Or maybe *she* was playing tricks on you.

You touch the apple in your pocket as your stomach churns with hunger. You wish you had more apples. More food. You don't know how long you'll be out here.

7

Just as you are about to set off into the trees again, a shadow drops across your path. You crouch down as it looms closer. What if it's her? You can't let her find you.

9

TO BE SECRET AGENT SNOW WORKING FOR GOOD PRINCE IN A
FUTURISTIC WORLD,
TURN TO PAGE 11.

TO BE A STEPMOTHER SEARCHING FOR YOUR RUNAWAY
STEPDAUGHTER SNOW,
TURN TO PAGE 41.

TO LIVE IN THE ARCTIC WITH YOUR SEVEN LOYAL DOGS,
TURN TO PAGE 75.

## CHAPTER 2

# Secret Agent Snow and the Seven Robots

"Hunter? Come in, Hunter. White Snow here. Are you there?"

All you hear is crackling on the other end. You hold up your phone to catch a better signal. But the woods are thick and overgrown, and you are far from any cell tower.

You head toward a small clearing you remember passing. Even though you've gotten separated from your partner Hunter, the mission is still the same. Find the Apple.

11

A war is on between Good Prince and Evil Queen. For many years Good Prince has been ruler of this land. Under his reign homelessness decreased, every child received a good education, and the land was at peace.

That is until Evil Queen rose to power as second-in-command. Evil Queen is greedy and power-hungry. To gain followers she promises them power and riches, but she never actually delivers. She even captures the homeless off the streets and forces them to become her servants, keeping her palace clean and her jewels sparkling.

Now Evil Queen has launched an all-out war to overthrow Good Prince. You are a secret agent in Good Prince's army. Your code name is White Snow.

Just last night Good Prince called you and Hunter to C.A.S.T.L.E., his underground intelligence bunker. He flipped on the large screen in front of you. On the screen was a red-colored object that looked like a computer monitor, but it wasn't flat. Instead it had a bulbous tube rounding from its back. A large, boat-shaped keyboard jutted from the bottom. You mentally took note of all its characteristics while Good Prince explained.

"This is Apple 2E," he said.

"It looks like an ancient relic!" Hunter exclaimed.

Good Prince went on. "This computer contains a secret code for a bomb. We need to find it before Evil Queen and her cronies do. If they find it first, they could launch the bomb and destroy us all."

The intelligence report indicated that
the last signal received from Apple 2E came
from Charming Woods, a vast forest covering
hundreds of miles. It's where Evil Queen and
her cronies hide out. You and Hunter set off
immediately. But now you've gotten separated,
and he's not answering your calls.

Once you reach the clearing, you catch a signal
and open your trusty spy app, Mirror. It contains
a GPS map and can communicate with other
agents. Just as you are about to make contact, you
hear a crash in the woods behind you. It could be
Hunter. Or it could be one of Evil Queen's goons.

You run through the woods and hide behind
a tree. You can still hear something behind you.
You touch the apple in your pocket. You wish
that you had more. You don't know when you'll
get a chance to eat a full meal again.

Just as you're about to creep through the trees again, you see a shadow on the ground in front of you. What if it's Evil Queen? You stand still, hoping to blend into the trees. If she sees you, you're doomed.

The shadow moves on, and you let out a sigh of relief. Suddenly you hear the sound of footsteps. They are walking away from you. You could walk toward the sound to see if it's Hunter. Or you could stay hidden.

TO WALK TOWARD THE FOOTSTEPS,
TURN TO PAGE 16.

TO STAY HIDDEN,
TURN TO PAGE 19.

You silently slip through the trees. Your secret-agent training has taught you how to move without making a sound. As you move toward the sound of the footsteps, you hear Hunter's voice booming through the woods. You rush toward the sound and see him leaning against a tree. He's shouting into his phone.

"No, please! I did exactly as you asked," he cries. "She vanished. I've looked everywhere!"

Suddenly your phone buzzes in your pocket. You wish you had silenced it. Hunter stops talking and glances in your direction. His face reddens, and he quickly puts the phone behind his back.

"White Snow!" he says, relieved. "I've been looking for you. I'm glad you're safe. It's dangerous out here."

"Who were you talking to?" you ask.

"Umm . . . a friend. I mean a confidential informant," he says. "We have a lead on Apple."

You wonder why Hunter's being secretive, but he must have a good reason. "We need to stop wasting time and get moving," you say.

You glance at your phone and see a notification from the Mirror app: POSSIBLE SIGNAL SOUTH, the message reads.

"This way," Hunter says, pointing north. "My intel says this will lead us to Apple 2E."

"Mirror says south," you tell him.

But Hunter has started off into the trees. "Come on!" he says.

You start to follow him, then stop. Maybe you'll find Apple 2E faster if you split up.

TO GO WITH HUNTER,
TURN TO PAGE 22.

TO HEAD SOUTH ON YOUR OWN,
TURN TO PAGE 24.

You decide to stay hidden. You can't risk being caught by the enemy. If it's Hunter, you'll find each other eventually.

You listen as the footsteps fade then grow louder again. Whoever it is seems to be walking in circles. As the footsteps grow closer, birds scatter from branches above you. You hear a rabbit scurrying away. Even the animals are spooked. You make yourself as small as possible behind the tree in order to blend in.

*Crunch! Crunch! Crunch!* The footsteps stop near your hiding spot. You hold your breath. You have no idea if the person can see you. You can only cross your fingers and hope. A long, silent moment passes. Then a strong hand reaches out and grabs your arm.

19

TURN THE PAGE.

"Ahh!" you cry as you try to spin around. You catch a glimpse of your attacker's face. You know him. Relief floods you. Then he claps a hand over your mouth.

"Hey! What are you doing?" you try to say, but your words are muffled by his hand.

"You and me, we're going on a little trip to see Evil Queen," he says.

You struggle, but he keeps pushing you through the trees. You hear a sound that you recognize. It's his cell phone. He pulls it from his pocket. You struggle even harder, hoping that you can wriggle free. But his hold is strong.

"What?" he says into the phone. "Yeah, I've got her. You want just the heart? No, that wasn't the deal. If you want it, you can take it." He clicks off the phone and continues pushing you through the woods.

21

"Evil Queen wants your heart. There's no hope for you now," he cackles as he takes you to Evil Queen's castle.

## THE END

TO FOLLOW ANOTHER PATH, TURN TO PAGE 9.

You follow Hunter through the trees. The sky is darkening, and Hunter's path is winding. You no longer know which direction you're going. You feel lost and are out of breath trying to keep up.

"Hunter," you gasp, "are you sure this is the right way?"

"The clue is just ahead!" he insists.

As you take another exhausted step behind him, your pant leg catches on something. You reach down to pull it free, when a metal hand grasps your finger.

*A metal hand?* you think. You look down, straight into the eyes of a tiny robot.

"What—" you start to say, but the robot holds its finger to its mouth to shush you.

The robot points at a screen on its chest with the message: I WORK FOR GOOD PRINCE. FOLLOW ME. DON'T SAY A WORD.

*This might be a trap,* you think. You know you are in the midst of Evil Queen's territory. But still you are curious. The robot is so small that you could easily overpower it if things get sketchy.

"You coming?" Hunter calls. You can no longer see him. You can only hear his voice in the distance.

23

TO FOLLOW THE ROBOT,
TURN TO PAGE 28.

TO CONTINUE FOLLOWING HUNTER,
TURN TO PAGE 31.

"You go your way, and I'll go mine," you call out to Hunter. "Let me know if you find anything."

You head south. The trees grow thicker. You are glad you have Mirror's GPS, otherwise you'd never find your way around.

Suddenly your phone chirps. The battery is low. You reach in your pack for the portable charger. With a sinking feeling, you realize Hunter has it. You are out here alone with a dead phone. You continue walking until you see something shimmering in the distance. You head toward it and discover a small, metal door on the side of the hill.

"Hmm," you say. "An abandoned mine shaft?" You push open the door and peer into pitch darkness. You can't see a thing. Apple 2E could be anywhere. You have to check inside.

You wriggle through the door and look around. You are standing in a large, round room with seven small, metal beds. Each one is connected to an outlet.

"Hmm, that's strange," you say to yourself.

You scan the room for Apple 2E. It's not here, but you do see a pile of cords and electronics next to one of the beds. You sort through the pile. Eventually you find a charger and plug in your phone. You sit down on a metal bed to wait. Suddenly you notice a strange smell wafting around you.

*What is that?* you wonder. You try to stand up, but it's too late. You're already falling into a deep sleep.

*Beep! Beep! Beep!* The sound jolts you awake. You sit up and see seven small robots surrounding you.

"What are you doing in our docking station?" one of them yells.

Another robot swivels toward you and scans your face. "Identified as Agent White Snow."

"Hello, Agent," the robot says. "We work for Good Prince. I'm Doc Bot, and this is Happy Bot, Bashful Bot, Dopey Bot, Sneezy Bot, Sleepy Bot, and Grumpy Bot."

*Allies, what luck!* you think. You nod hello.

Just then there's a sharp knock on the door. An old woman's voice calls out, "Hello? Anyone home? I have a message for Agent Snow."

You start toward the door, but the robots block your way. "Don't open it," Doc Bot cautions. "It could be a trap."

"Let's go out the back door and search for Apple 2E instead," Sneezy Bot agrees.

27

The robots may be able to help you find Apple 2E. But what if the message is important?

TO LEAVE WITH THE ROBOTS, TURN TO PAGE 36.

TO OPEN THE DOOR, TURN TO PAGE 38.

Wordlessly you follow the robot as it whirs through a maze of trees. It leads you to a small door on the side of a hill. The door flies open and out tumbles another tiny robot, then another, and another. Seven robots in all!

"I'm Doc Bot," says the robot that found you. "And this is Sleepy Bot, Happy Bot, Sneezy Bot, Grumpy Bot, Dopey Bot, and Bashful Bot. We work for Good Prince."

In all your years working for Good Prince, you've never heard of these robots. You snap a quick photo of them and upload it to the

Mirror app.

The app reads: "VERIFIED AS ALLIES OF GOOD PRINCE. PLEASE PROCEED."

Doc Bot tells you that each robot has a special skill to help win the war against Evil Queen. Doc can give medical treatment. Sleepy Bot can make an enemy fall asleep. Sneezy Bot can blow poison goo from its nose. Happy Bot can change a person from evil to good. Dopey Bot can make a person forgetful. Bashful Bot can make someone hide in fear, and Grumpy Bot is a bomb that explodes when its face turns red.

"We need to work together to find Apple 2E," Doc Bot tells you. "And we know just where to begin."

"But what about my partner Hunter?" you ask.

The robots are silent for a moment. Then Happy Bot pipes up. "We don't think he can be trusted," it says.

As if on cue, your phone buzzes. It's a call from Hunter. "Come quickly!" he says. "I found something!"

"On my way," you say, and click the phone off. The robots are staring at you.

"Could it be a trap?" Doc Bot wonders.

You think for a moment. Hunter *was* acting strangely, leading you on a winding trail through the woods.

"Finding Apple 2E is of the highest importance," Sneezy Bot says.

30

You agree and think that Hunter could have a lead, even if he *might be* working for Evil Queen.

TO LEAVE AND FIND HUNTER, GO TO PAGE 31.

TO GO WITH THE ROBOTS, TURN TO PAGE 33.

You stomp through the woods to find Hunter. He's standing on the edge of a cliff.

"Hunter!" you call to him. "What is going on?"

He waves at you to come closer. When you reach his side, he points at something far ahead. Across the valley you see a tall, black palace on the top of a hill. You recognize it immediately.

"Evil Queen's palace!" you exclaim, turning to Hunter. "But what—"

Suddenly your voice has a sharp echo. You take a step toward Hunter but run into something solid. A glass wall. You turn in the other direction, but hit another glass wall. You realize with dread that you are trapped inside!

31

TURN THE PAGE.

You pound on the glass. "Hunter! What have you done?" you cry. Hunter only looks at you and smirks. You can't believe Hunter, your trusted partner, turned on you and Good Prince. "Traitor!" you shout.

"Take White Snow away!" Hunter calls into the air. Suddenly dozens of armed Evil Queen soldiers run out from the trees and lift the case. They tilt it sideways and you fall over, smacking your head hard against the glass. You see stars.

*It's like a glass coffin*, you think just as everything goes black. You are carried away as a prisoner of war.

## THE END

TO FOLLOW ANOTHER PATH, TURN TO PAGE 9.

You and the robots prowl through the woods looking for any sign of Apple 2E. As night comes you are about to give up until morning. Suddenly your Mirror app beeps. It reads: SIGNAL DETECTED. You and the robots scurry toward the location.

As you approach you see a figure in the trees. It's Evil Queen! The Apple 2E's screen glows with a greenish light in front of her.

"Curses!" Evil Queen mutters, punching the computer keys. "I can't crack the code!"

You see your chance. "Robots, attack!" you shout.

The robots lunge at Evil Queen, beeping angrily. Evil Queen is taken by surprise, but she doesn't look afraid. "You silly robots can't defeat me!" she screams.

"That's what you think, Evil Queen," you yell. "Dopey, let her have it!"

Dopey Bot takes aim and shoots a laser straight at the queen's forehead. Direct hit! The force knocks Evil Queen to the ground. She groans and struggles to sit up.

"Where am I? *Who* am I?" Evil Queen asks with one hand on her forehead. The other is still holding on to Apple 2E. "And what am I holding?"

"Oh you're holding that for me," you say quickly. "But I'll take it back now." You grab Apple 2E and hoist it up onto your shoulders. "Good Prince thanks you for your assistance."

"Um . . . sure. I mean of course! Anything to help a prince," Evil Queen says still confused.

You tell the robots to watch Evil Queen, and you head toward C.A.S.T.L.E. and Good Prince. Once there you are treated as a hero.

"Excellent work, Snow," Good Prince says. "You saved the day."

After you leave C.A.S.T.L.E., you pull out your phone. "Mirror, Mirror in my hand," you say. "Who is the greatest secret agent in the land?"

You read Mirror's answer loud and clear: SNOW, WHITE SNOW.

## THE END
TO FOLLOW ANOTHER PATH, TURN TO PAGE 9.

You and the robots hike into the woods. But as night falls, you get separated. You climb a small path to the top of a hill. As you near the top, you see an old woman crouched along the path holding an apple.

"Ah, Agent. I've been expecting you," she says as you come near. "I work for Good Prince. I have the item that you seek."

The woman steps away and reveals the Apple 2E behind her. You've found it! Good Prince will be so pleased.

"My, you must be famished," the woman says. "Here, I have an apple. Eat before you start your journey back to C.A.S.T.L.E."

You are a little hungry, but you need to get moving. "I'm sorry, I have to get back to Good Prince."

"How about half the apple then?" the old woman asks. She slices the apple with a small knife and gives one half to you. She bites into her half, licking her lips. "Delicious!" she says.

Watching the old woman eat makes you hungry. You take a bite of your apple half and swallow. Suddenly the old woman springs to her feet, cackling. She rips off her gray wig, revealing glossy, blond hair. It's Evil Queen in disguise!

"That's the last apple you'll ever eat!" she cries. A sharp pain pierces your gut.

"You poisoned me!" you exclaim as you fall to the ground. You can no longer feel your arms and legs. You fall into a deep, poisoned sleep as Evil Queen takes Apple 2E away.

37

## THE END

TO FOLLOW ANOTHER PATH, TURN TO PAGE 9.

Maybe the woman's message is important. Your phone has been dead this whole time. What if Good Prince has been trying to contact you?

You step around the robots and fling open the door. A woman with a scarf around her face hobbles in. Just as you are about to ask for the message, Sleepy Bot shoots the woman with its sleep tranquilizers. She slumps to the floor.

"What did you do?" you cry angrily. You run to the woman's side and pull her scarf from her face. It's not an old woman at all. It's Evil Queen!

38

"I told you it was a trap!" Grumpy Bot barks.

"That was close! Great work, robots," you say with relief as the robots tie up the sleeping queen.

Even though Evil Queen is no longer a threat, your work is not over. You still need to find Apple 2E and deliver it to Good Prince. You wonder if Hunter has had any luck.

"Thanks for your help!" You wave at the robots as you step out the door to the woods.

You reach for your phone, now fully charged, and call Hunter so you can search together. Now that Evil Queen has been captured, there's no hurry. You might even enjoy looking for Apple 2E now. You set off on your search, whistling while you work.

## THE END

TO FOLLOW ANOTHER PATH, TURN TO PAGE 9.

# Runaway Snow

You've just gotten home from a long day of work. Your stepdaughter Snow is nowhere in sight. She must be listening to rock music in her bedroom again. You decide not to bother her. You and Snow used to be very close. She even chose to live with you after you and her father split up. But lately Snow has been grouchy and sullen.

You decide to make an apple pie for her as a treat. Snow loves apples. You are just getting out the ingredients when the doorbell rings. At the door is Wally Mirror, a boy from Snow's class. He holds up his backpack.

4!

"I'm here to work on a group project with Snow," Wally tells you. You hope Wally will cheer Snow up. She has a huge crush on him, but Wally is completely clueless. You rush to Snow's bedroom to tell her. You knock on her door, but she doesn't answer. She must be wearing her headphones.

"Wally's here," you say, opening the door.

"What?" she yells.

"Can you take those off?" you shout, pointing to her ears.

42    "But this is my favorite Septuplets song!" she protests, pulling her headphones down.

"Wally's here," you repeat.

Snow turns to peer into the mirror over her dresser. She stares at her reflection and frowns. She doesn't think she's very pretty.

"My hair is too dark," Snow pouts. "My skin is too pale. My lips are too red."

"You're beautiful," you say.

Snow sighs then grabs her laptop and heads downstairs where Wally is waiting. Wally and Snow sit at the kitchen table to work on the project while you continue making the pie.

Wally turns to Snow and whispers, "Wow, your stepmom is *so* pretty. I bet she's the prettiest person in town!"

Snow slams her laptop shut. "Let's finish tomorrow," she says irritably.

**43**

Wally looks surprised. "Um, OK. See you—"

"Yeah, bye," Snow interrupts, then runs up to her room and slams the door.

After Wally leaves you knock on Snow's door. She flings it open, tears streaming down her face.

"It's all your fault!" Snow yells. "You're the pretty one. Not me! I can't live here anymore." She grabs her duffel bag and pushes past you down the hall and out the front door.

"Wait!" you cry running after her, but Snow doesn't slow down.

By the time you reach the sidewalk, you don't see Snow anywhere. You think she might have gone to the nearby woods to hide. It was always her favorite place as a little girl. You run as fast as you can into the woods. You touch the apple in your pocket as your stomach churns with hunger. You never did get a chance to eat that pie.

Just as you are about to set off into the trees again, a shadow drops across your path. It grows bigger and bigger. Two faces peer around a tree trunk at you. It's your neighbor's boys, Will and Jacob Grimm.

"Hey, Ms. White!" they exclaim. "What are you doing out here?"

"Looking for Snow," you tell them. "Have you seen her?"

The Grimm brothers look at each other. "She said she was running away and never coming back," Jacob finally mumbles.

"Do you know where she's going?" you ask.

"Didn't say," Will answers.

You know you need to find Snow before she gets too far. She could be at Fairy Park, her favorite park in the city. But if she *really* wants to run away, she might be at the train station. It's the fastest way out of town.

TO SEARCH IN FAIRY PARK,
GO TO PAGE 47.

TO GO TO THE TRAIN STATION,
TURN TO PAGE 50.

You decide to head downtown and search Fairy Park. The park stretches over several city blocks. You'd forgotten how huge the park is. Snow could be anywhere.

You enter the gates. The park is jam-packed with people carrying drinks, eating food, and having a good time. On a stage at the far end of the park, a rock band is playing. You tap someone on the shoulder.

"What's going on?" you ask.

"Fairy Fest," he yells over the music. "The park's biggest music fair."

"Oh, no," you groan. It's going to be much more difficult to find Snow amongst all these people. But you are also relieved. Snow loves music, so she's bound to be here somewhere. But where?

As you move through the crowd, the band on stage begins a new song. The band looks familiar, but you can't quite place them. Then you realize you've seen their poster hanging on Snow's bedroom wall. It's the Septuplets, her favorite band!

*The Septuplets could help me find Snow,* you think.

You elbow through the crowd to get closer to the stage. You still have a long way to go when the song ends. Oh, no! The band is starting to pack up their equipment. You try to move faster, but the huge crowd is tough to push through. At this rate you might never catch the band.

As you move through the crowd, vendors call out to you trying to sell their goods — fresh fruit, beautiful hair combs, and band T-shirts.

You are struck with an idea. Snow has never been able to resist food and shiny trinkets. You could pose as a vendor and bring her right to you. Or you could keep trying to catch the Septuplets.

TO POSE AS A VENDOR SELLING ITEMS, TURN TO PAGE 52.

TO KEEP GOING TOWARD THE SEPTUPLETS, TURN TO PAGE 54.

You know that if Snow is determined to run away, she'll try to get as far away as possible. The train station is the best place to look. You have to catch her before she has a chance to board a train.

When you reach the station, you are amazed at how big it is. You stare at the huge monitors that list all the departures. Which train would she take?

You approach the ticket counter and pull out a picture of Snow. "Have you seen this girl?" you ask the two ticket attendants.

The male attendant peers at the photograph and shrugs. "I don't remember."

The female attendant points at something behind you. "Maybe you should ask him," she suggests.

You whirl around. On the wall behind you is a poster of a man in a suit holding a magnifying glass. It reads:

*On the hunt for someone?*

*Call Theo Huntsman, Private Investigator.*

You could use help finding Snow. But you still might be able to find her on your own.

51

TO CALL THEO HUNTSMAN, TURN TO PAGE 64.

TO SEARCH THE TRAIN STATION ON YOUR OWN, TURN TO PAGE 67.

You decide to try luring Snow to you by selling the things she loves. You walk toward the vendor stands lined up on the edge of the park.

"Apples and fruits galore!" one seller calls out.

"Get your beautiful jeweled combs here!" another hollers.

You approach the fruit stand and comb sellers. "Would either of you like a break?" you ask. "I could take over for a while. I'm a good salesperson!"

"I would love a break!" the fruit seller exclaims.

"So would I!" says the comb seller. "I've been here all day."

You look from one to the other. Your stepdaughter absolutely loves apples, and she's probably hungry. But she'd also want a shiny, jeweled comb for her hair.

53

TO SELL FRUIT,
TURN TO PAGE 59.

TO SELL JEWELED COMBS,
TURN TO PAGE 61.

You decide to try to catch the Septuplets before they leave the park. You weave through the crowd of people toward the stage, ignoring the cries of vendors and stepping on people's toes. Finally, breathless, you reach the stage just as the band members have loaded the last of their stuff into an old wood-paneled van.

"Wait!" you cry.

The Septuplets stop and turn toward you. One band member stretches her arms out and yawns. Another sneezes.

A third smiles at you. "Hello!" she says.

Another girl sighs and rolls her eyes. "Oh great, another fan who wants an autograph. Let's just go."

"No, no, I'm not a fan," you say.

The seven girls stare at you. Your cheeks flush with embarrassment. "I mean . . . that's not why I'm here. I need your help." You tell the Septuplets about Snow, Wally, and the whole misunderstanding.

"Oh, that's awful!" one Septuplet says. "We'd love to help."

You sigh, relieved. The girls introduce themselves as Coy, Bliss, Simple, Dozy, Snappy, Medic, and Sniffle.

The girls start brainstorming ideas. "We could write a song telling Snow to come home," Simple offers.

"That would take too long," Snappy argues.

"I say search the wooded area of Fairy Park. She's probably hiding," Coy says from behind her long bangs.

"Throw a party!" Bliss suggests cheerily. "She'll definitely come home for a party."

Your mind is reeling. All the girls have great suggestions, but you don't know which one would be the best.

TO TAKE BLISS' ADVICE, AND THROW A PARTY,
GO TO PAGE 57.

TO TAKE COY'S ADVICE, AND SEARCH THE WOODS,
TURN TO PAGE 70.

You decide to throw a party, and you invite the Septuplets to play in your backyard. You know Snow would never be able to resist a party, especially if her favorite band is playing. You'll even make her favorite apple tarts. The Septuplets help you hang flyers around town. You call Ethan Printz, Snow's good friend, and tell him to post details of the party online.

The day of the party, you bake seven apple tarts. The smell of the sweet desserts wafts through the air. The Septuplets rock out in your backyard, and the house fills with people. Ethan Printz is there, along with Snow's other friends. Even the Grimm brothers show up to write about the party on their blog.

57

TURN THE PAGE.

Finally the door opens, and Snow walks in. "Whoa! Is that really the Septuplets playing in our yard?" she asks.

You wrap her in a big hug. "I threw this party just for you!" you tell her.

"Thanks!" she says. Then she frowns. "Is Wally Mirror here?" she asks.

"Forget him," you say. "You don't need a boy to tell you that you're beautiful and loved."

Snow gobbles up a piece of tart and goes out to the yard to dance. You watch her, smiling.

58  Maybe now you can all live happily ever after.

# THE END

TO FOLLOW ANOTHER PATH, TURN TO PAGE 9.

You tell the fruit seller to take a break and take her place behind the fruit stand. You pull a hat low over your face and conceal yourself with bushels of apples. You scan the crowd. You don't see a single person who looks like Snow.

"Apples! Fresh-picked apples!" you call shrilly, disguising your voice as much as you can. "Red ones, green ones. Tart and juicy!"

You hope that somewhere in the crowd, Snow will hear you and come running. All the yelling is making your throat hurt.

Suddenly you spot Snow wandering past. "Miss! Miss!" you cry in a squeaky voice. "A free apple for you, the fairest of them all!"

Snow stops and turns to you. You dangle the apple in front of you. Snow moves toward you and reaches for the apple.

59

You drop the apple into Snow's hand, revealing your face. "Snow, please come home," you say.

Snow rolls her eyes. "Oh, it's you," she says, eating the apple. "Fine, I'll come home. But only if I can bring my friends." She gestures behind her, and the entire Septuplets band comes forward. "They need a practice space," Snow tells you excitedly. "I told them our basement would be perfect!"

You are happy to have Snow home again, but you are not so happy about the Septuplets practicing in your basement. Your whole house rocks long into the night. But that's not even the worst part. A lot of their songs seem to involve whistling, which is really getting on your nerves.

## THE END

TO FOLLOW ANOTHER PATH, TURN TO PAGE 9.

Snow loves wearing shiny combs and barrettes in her hair. You figure she'll be drawn to the jeweled comb booth.

"I'll take your place for a while," you tell the comb seller. You hop into the stand and decorate your hair with beautiful combs. Then you wrap a scarf around your face and scan the crowd.

"Jeweled combs for sale!" you call, disguising your voice. Finally you see Snow moving through the crowd. "Hello there, Miss!" you cry. "Would you like to try on some jewelry?"

As Snow turns you see that she is already wearing several jeweled combs in her hair. Still she marches toward the stand. You are overjoyed until you see the angry look on her face.

"You can't fool me," she snaps. "I know it's you."

You slowly unwrap the scarf from your face and sigh. "Come home, Snow," you plead.

Snow shakes her head. "Not a chance!" she says. "I'm going to stay with Dad for a while."

Snow twirls away toward the fruit stand and buys a sketchy-looking apple. You sigh miserably. You hope she doesn't end up with food poisoning.

## THE END

TO FOLLOW ANOTHER PATH, TURN TO PAGE 9.

You know you need all the help you can get. You dial Theo Huntsman's number and wait for him to pick up.

"Huntsman, at your service," he says.

You explain the situation, and he tells you to come to his office. When you arrive he writes down your information and places it on top of one of the many piles on his desk. You wonder how he can keep track of anything.

"I'll call you with any leads," he says.

The next morning Theo Huntsman calls you to come to his office. "I've found something!" he says.

When you get to his office, you see that he's holding a small box. You reach for it, but he shoves it behind his back. "Fifty bucks," he says.

You hand him the money, and he opens the box. He holds up a necklace with a heart-shaped pendant.

"What is this?" you ask.

"That's Snow's heart," he tells you, "from the woods."

You shake your head. "No. This isn't Snow's," you say.

Theo Huntsman frowns. "What are you talking about? Of course this belongs to Snow."

You shake your head again. "I think I'd know Snow's heart when I see it."

"Oh," Theo says. "Well if you want me to keep searching, I'll need more money for expenses."

You aren't sure Theo Huntsman is worth the money you've paid him. But he may be your only hope. The only other option is to conduct your own search. The woods by Fairy Park would be a good place to start. It's Snow's favorite park.

66

TO SEARCH FAIRY PARK YOURSELF,
TURN TO PAGE 70.

TO PAY THEO HUNTSMAN TO KEEP SEARCHING,
TURN TO PAGE 72.

You don't have time to waste if you want to find Snow. You start running toward the departure train platforms.

"Ma'am!" the male attendant calls after you. "You need a ticket first!"

You ignore him and leap over the barricades. You hear the attendant's footsteps behind you, but you soon lose him in the crowd of passengers waiting for their trains. You wave a picture of Snow in people's faces.

"Have you seen this girl?" you ask. A tall man looks at the photo and points to a train about to depart. As you are about to run, you stop.

*How am I going to get Snow off the train?* you wonder. Just then you see one of Snow's friends, Ethan Printz. You've got an idea.

"Ethan, over here!" you say, waving the boy down. Ethan strides toward you, looking confident and regal.

"Hi, Ms. White. What's wrong?" Ethan asks. You tell him that Snow is running away on the train. You point toward it as the whistle blows.

"Hurry! It's departing!" you cry.

Ethan walks briskly toward the train. You follow, trying to stay out of sight. You can see Snow through the train's glass window. She's slumped in her seat, fast asleep. The train slowly pulls out of the station. Ethan holds up his hand, and the train squeals to a stop. The conductor leaps off the train. That's right! You forgot the Printz family owns most of the train lines.

From behind a pillar, you watch as Ethan steps aboard. You see him reach Snow and gently wake her up. As the pair leaves the train, you swear you see a spark between them.

*I guess it doesn't matter what Wally Mirror thinks after all,* you think.

69

## THE END
TO FOLLOW ANOTHER PATH, TURN TO PAGE 9.

You decide to search the woods in Fairy Park. Snow has always loved the woods. You take a deep breath and enter. You hope there aren't any wild animals here. Your eyes dart about, watching for any sign of Snow.

"Snow! Where are you?" you shout.

Then you hear someone singing. You move toward the sound. As you peer through the trees, you see Snow on a tree swing. The Grimm brothers are taking turns pushing her. She's singing to the squirrels that leap from branch to branch. You step out from behind the trees.

"Snow!" you cry. Snow jumps off the swing and starts to run away. "Wait! Please come home!" you beg.

Snow pauses, considering. You dig in your pocket and find your apple. You hand it to her.

Snow smiles. "An apple! My favorite! I am pretty hungry." She snatches the apple and devours it happily.

As she eats you approach the Grimm brothers. "Did you know where she was this whole time?" you demand.

The brothers shrug guiltily. "We just wanted to help her," one says.

"We were going to write about her adventures in our blog," the other adds.

You shake your head at them. "Come on, Snow," you say. "Let's go home."

## THE END

TO FOLLOW ANOTHER PATH, TURN TO PAGE 9.

You would pay anything to have Snow back. You hand over more money to Theo Huntsman. "I'll do what I can," he promises.

Several days pass. Then you receive a letter from Theo Huntsman. "I found her!" is written on the envelope.

You tear open the letter. Inside is a postcard of a castle nestled on a mountaintop. You flip the postcard over and see Snow's handwriting. The card is addressed to you. You sigh thinking of all the money you gave Theo Huntsman for a postcard that would have come to you anyway.

It reads: *Dear Mom,*

*Guess what? I'm living in a castle! It's really a school for girls. Dad enrolled me. I feel like a princess! Maybe you can visit someday.*

*Love, Snow.*

Someday seems so far away. You hang the postcard on the fridge and sigh again. At least Snow is living happily ever after.

## THE END

TO FOLLOW ANOTHER PATH, TURN TO PAGE 9.

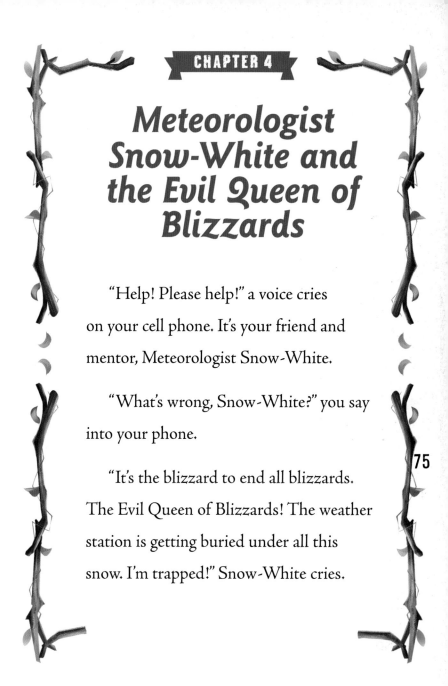

## CHAPTER 4

# Meteorologist Snow-White and the Evil Queen of Blizzards

"Help! Please help!" a voice cries on your cell phone. It's your friend and mentor, Meteorologist Snow-White.

"What's wrong, Snow-White?" you say into your phone.

"It's the blizzard to end all blizzards. The Evil Queen of Blizzards! The weather station is getting buried under all this snow. I'm trapped!" Snow-White cries.

"On my way!" you say. Snow-White has been teaching you everything she knows about weather. One day you hope to be a meteorologist just like her. Plus she's your best friend. You have to help her.

You take a peek out the window. All you can see is a sea of white. But that's not unusual since you and your family, the Charmings, live in the Arctic. You live far from civilization. The only way to get anywhere is by dogsled.

Your seven sled dogs are stretched out on their seven beds in front of the fireplace. You've raised the dogs since you found them as puppies, abandoned in an old cottage. They all look alike, but you can tell them apart. You named them based on their personalities: Doc, Grumpy, Bashful, Sleepy, Sneezy, Dopey, and Happy. Doc is the lead dog and always takes care of the others.

You bundle up and whistle for the dogs to wake up. The dogs leap to attention, except for Sleepy. She just rolls over and buries her face in her paws. You give her a gentle nudge.

When the dogs are ready, you open the door and step out into the bitter wind. The Evil Queen of Blizzards hasn't reached your house yet, but you can see the storm coming your way. You know Snow-White's weather station is in the thick of the storm. You need to get to her quickly. She's all alone out there.

You and the dogs traipse through the woods near your house. The trees are too thick to ride the sled, so you pull it behind you. The sky darkens. All you can hear is your own breathing and the dogs panting as you quicken your pace through the trees. You think you hear something behind you. You imagine the Evil Queen of Blizzards looming over you, ready to touch down and bury you in a mountain of snow. You duck behind a tree to catch your breath.

All you hear is silence now. Maybe your mind was playing tricks on you. You touch the apple in your pocket as your stomach churns with hunger. You wish you had more apples. More food. You don't know how long you'll be out here.

You start off again into the trees, the dogs at your heels. When you reach the trail to the weather station, you leash the dogs to the front of the sled. Before you hop on, you pull out your binoculars.

*Uh-oh*, you think. The storm is right in your path. You could take another trail around it, but then you risk not getting to Snow-White in time.

TO GO AROUND THE STORM,
TURN TO PAGE 80.

TO TAKE THE DIRECT PATH TO SNOW-WHITE,
TURN TO PAGE 82.

You decide it's too dangerous to venture straight into the path of the storm. Your storm-watching skills tell you that you could head east, where the storm is weakest. Then you could double-back to the weather station.

You shake the dogs' reins and they run across the small rolling hills. Even though the storm is weaker to the east, the wind is still harsh and stirs up snow. It is nearly blinding. The dogs strain to pull you through the terrible wind. As you round a hill, you spot dark, moving shapes in the distance.

"Whoa," you say to the dogs. They slow to a stop, and you take out your binoculars again. A group of men is coming over the hills on horseback. The leader is carrying a flag with a large "H" on it.

At the sight of the flag, your heart freezes in your chest. It's the Huntsmen, a notorious gang of roving thieves. They are legendary and vicious — robbing homes and travelers. They'll take anything they can get their hands on. You know that if they find you, they'll take your dogs and your sled. They'll probably even take the half-eaten apple in your pocket.

You peer through the binoculars again. The Huntsmen are headed straight toward you. You remember seeing a cave a little ways back where you and the dogs could hide. Or you could try to outrun them.

TO HIDE IN THE CAVE,
TURN TO PAGE 84.

TO MAKE A RUN FOR IT,
TURN TO PAGE 99.

You need to get to Snow-White as quickly as possible. The most direct path is through the storm. You snap the dogs' reins and plunge forward.

The wind howls and the snow swirls as you push on through the storm. The snow is so thick, you can barely see the dogs a few feet in front of you. The icy snow stings your eyes and face. You stop to rub your eyes with your glove. Suddenly you see something moving in front of you. You look sideways and see an apple rolling away across the ice.

*An apple?* you think. You peer into the distance and see what looks like huge crates of apples. Why would all those apples be out here in the Arctic? Are you dreaming?

Then you hear a voice up ahead. "Where are you?" someone shouts. "I can't see anything!"

"Over here!" says another voice.

This time you know it's not your imagination. These people could be lost out here in the storm. Maybe you could help them. Then again Snow-White is still in danger. You think of the crates of apples. You could use the food and so could Snow-White.

TO HEAD TOWARD THE VOICES,
TURN TO PAGE 87.

TO CHECK OUT THE APPLES,
TURN TO PAGE 90.

You decide to head toward the cave. It's hidden from view, and the Huntsmen aren't likely to find you there.

You and the dogs duck inside. It is pitch black, and you can't see a thing. Your dogs huddle around you for warmth. Then Grumpy starts growling and straining at his leash. Bashful hides his face in his paws and whines.

You click on your flashlight to see what the fuss is about. The cave is lined with treasures — gold, jewelry, furs, and stacks of money. With dread you realize you are in the Huntsmen's hideout. It's too late to run. You hear the Huntsmen at the cave's entrance. You pull the dogs to the corner of the cave out of sight and tell them to stay. There's no way you're letting the Huntsmen take them.